D0855095

Creatures of the Deep

GIANT TUBE WORMS
AND OTHER INTERESTING INVERTEBRATES

Heidi Moore

Riverhead Free Library
330 Court Street
Riverhead, New York 11901

Raintree

Chicago, Illinois

www.heinemannraintree.com
Visit our website to find out more information about Heinemann-Raintree books.

To order:

☎ Phone 888-454-2279

💻 Visit www.heinemannraintree.com to browse our catalog and order online.

©2012 Raintree
an imprint of Capstone Global Library, LLC
Chicago, Illinois

All rights reserved. No part of this publication may be reproduced or transmitted in any form or by any means, electronic or mechanical, including photocopying, recording, taping, or any information storage and retrieval system, without permission in writing from the publisher.

Edited by Megan Cotugno and Abby Colich
Designed by Philippa Jenkins
Illustrated by Terry Pastor / www.theartagency.co.uk
Picture research by Hannah Taylor
Originated by Capstone Global Library
Printed and bound in China by CTPS

15 14 13 12 11
10 9 8 7 6 5 4 3 2 1

Library of Congress Cataloging-in-Publication Data

Moore, Heidi, 1976-
  Giant tube worms and other interesting invertebrates / Heidi Moore.—1st ed.
     p. cm.—(Creatures of the deep)
  Includes bibliographical references and index.
  ISBN 978-1-4109-4199-2 (hc)—ISBN 978-1-4109-4206-7 (pb) 1. Marine invertebrates—Juvenile literature. I. Title.
  QL365.363.M66 2012
  592'.177—dc22   2010038393

Acknowledgments
We would like to thank the following for permission to reproduce photographs:

© Kevin Raskoff/ MBARI p. 22; Corbis pp. 8 (© Ralph White), 25, 26 (© Bettmann); FLPA p. 6 (Minden Pictures/ Norbert Wu); Image Quest Marine pp. 12, 15, 17, 18, 20, 21, 29; naturepl.com pp. 24, 28 (David Shale); NOAA p. 27; Photolibrary pp. 5 (Phototake Science/ Kathleen Crane), 10, 19 (OSF/ Scripps Inst Oceanography); Photoshot p. 4; Science Photo Library p. 14 (Thierry Berrod, Mona Lisa Production); SeaPics.com p. 23 (Lia Barrett); Shutterstock p. 7 (© Jeffrey M. Frank)

Cover photograph of Giant Tubeworm Colony reproduced with permission of Corbis (Ralph White).

We would like to thank Michael Bright for his invaluable help in the preparation of this book.

Every effort has been made to contact copyright holders of material reproduced in this book. Any omissions will be rectified in subsequent printings if notice is given to the publisher.

All the Internet addresses (URLs) given in this book were valid at the time of going to press. However, due to the dynamic nature of the Internet, some addresses may have changed, or sites may have changed or ceased to exist since publication. While the author and publisher regret any inconvenience this may cause readers, no responsibility for any such changes can be accepted by either the author or the publisher.

CONTENTS

Some words are printed in bold, **like this**. You can find out what they mean by looking in the glossary.

GIANT TUBE WORMS

In 1977 a group of scientists made an amazing discovery. They were exploring the deep sea at depths of about 2,500 meters (8,200 feet). This was near the Galapagos Islands in the Pacific Ocean.

Underwater springs

In this cold, dark place, the scientists found hot **springs**! The springs come from underwater vents, or gaps in the ocean floor. These vents spew out, or release, heat, steam, and gases from deep within the earth. Before this, scientists thought no living things could survive here. But they found many deep-sea dwellers living near the vents. There were huge clams, blind shrimp, and white crabs.

A deep-sea explorer takes pictures of life in the deep.

Giant tube worms live near deep sea vents.

Monster worm?

One of the most unusual creatures found near the vents was the giant tube worm. It is a large white worm with a red plume at the top. The plume is a feathery part that sits on top of the body. Giant tube worms can grow up to 2.4 meters (8 feet). This is taller than a person!

Field of Flowers

With their red plumes, a swaying cluster of giant tube worms looks like poppies waving in the breeze. Some people think they look like tubes of lipstick.

LIFE IN THE DEEP SEA

Life in the deep sea is difficult. Little to no sunlight makes its way down there. At some depths, there is total darkness. The water is very cold. There is also intense water **pressure**. The farther below the surface, the harder it is to survive.

Adaptations

Many deep ocean dwellers have **adapted** to this tough **habitat**. They have unique features that help them survive far below the surface. Some creatures, such as deep-sea shrimp, make their own light. Special chemicals (substances) in their bodies glow. This is called **bioluminescence**. Have you ever seen fireflies at night? They have bioluminescence, too.

This comb jelly glows with bioluminesence.

Lake Tahoe in the western U.S. is a fresh-water habitat.

Freshwater, Salt Water

Freshwater is found in lakes and rivers. It contains little salt. Seas and oceans have salt water. These are known as **marine** bodies. Oceans cover about 70 percent of Earth's surface. They are important habitats that are home to many amazing creatures.

DEEP-SEA VENTS

Deep-sea vents are a strange place to call home. These are very harsh **marine habitats**.

This vent spews out black smoke.

Hot and cold

Hydrothermal vents have extremes of heat and cold. The word hydrothermal means "hot water." Water from the vents can be close to boiling. That is hot enough to cook an egg in a few minutes! But nearby the water is very cold.

Poisonous gases

Hydrothermal vents spew many gases, such as hydrogen sulfide. Some of these gases are **toxic**, or poisonous. The vent openings range in size from 13 millimeters (0.5 inch) to more than 1.8 meters (6 feet).

Animals living near the vents **adapt** to these unique conditions. So far, scientists know about more than 300 types of creatures that survive near hydrothermal vents! Somehow these creatures do not get cooked by the hot temperatures.

Underwater Chimneys

Some hydrothermal vents are called black smokers. They spit out black smoke like chimneys. Sometimes iron in the smoke stains the tube worms orange!

BOOM OR BUST

Scientists once thought that it would be too hot to survive near **hydrothermal** vents. But the heat they provide can mean life or death for some creatures.

On and off

Sometimes these vents switch on and off. When the vent stops spewing gas, the animals cannot survive. When the vent switches back on, new animals move in. They grow very quickly. These animals have learned how to take advantage of the right conditions.

Tube Worm Barbecue

Scientists found one extremely hot hydrothermal vent in the Pacific Ocean. They recorded temperatures up to 403°C (757°F). The water was so hot it burned the giant tube worms' flesh. So scientists named this site Tube Worm Barbecue.

Plant-Free Zone

There is no sunlight deep in the ocean. That means plants cannot grow there. Plants need sunlight to make their own food.

Sulfide-Rich Hot Water

Vent Fish

Vent

Vent

Octopus

Giant Tubeworms

Galatheid Crabs

Many living things make their home near a vent.

Limpets

Giant White Clams

A giant tube worm is pretty much what it sounds like. It is mostly a tube.

The body of a tube worm

Giant tube worms have three main parts. Its main part is a long, thin, worm-like body. This part sits inside a tube made of a hard material called **chitin**. The third part is the plume, which sits on top of the body. The plume is red because it is filled with blood.

Giant tube worms do not have a stomach or a mouth. They also do not have eyes. There is no need for eyes in the deep ocean. After all, there is no sunlight down there.

The red plume atop a tube worm's body is filled with blood.

Baby tube worms

Tube worms produce new tube worms by **spawning**. A tube worm releases **sperm** and eggs into the water. The sperm and egg combine to create a new tube worm. After it hatches, the tiny tube worm swims down to a rock and attaches there to grow.

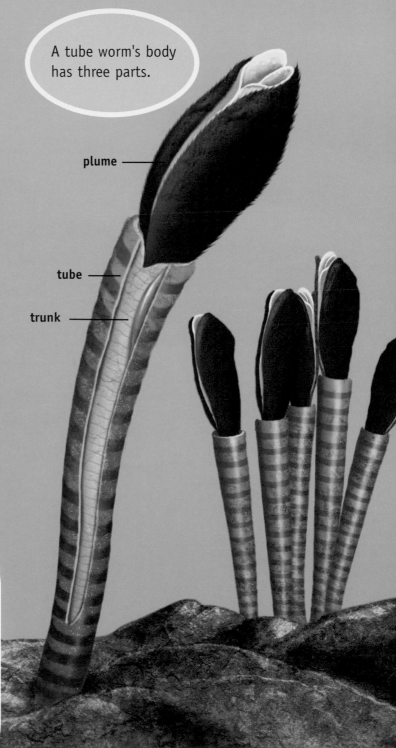

A tube worm's body has three parts.

plume

tube

trunk

Fast Growing

Giant tube worms grow quickly. They can grow up to 84 centimeters (33 inches) per year.

POISON FOR FOOD

Giant tube worms do not have a mouth or gut. So how do they eat food? The answer is that they don't! But they still need a source of **energy**.

Giant tube worms' energy comes from hydrogen sulfide. This is one of the gases a **hydrothermal** vent releases. You might have smelled hydrogen sulfide before. It often wafts out of sewers and smells like rotten eggs. Hydrogen sulfide is very **toxic** (poisonous) to humans. But to **bacteria** living near the vent, it is food! Vent bacteria use hydrogen sulfide to make energy. The bacteria, in turn, supply energy to the deep-sea dwellers living there.

This is a close-up image of bacteria.

Getting energy

This process happens inside a giant tube worm's body! A tube worm is filled with squishy brown tissue loaded with bacteria. Blood inside the tube worm's plume takes in hydrogen sulfide and then sends it down to bacteria in the tissue. The bacteria feed on the hydrogen sulfide and produce energy for the tube worm. The giant tube worm lives off of poison!

This tube worm lives near a hydrothermal vent.

POMPEII WORMS

There are many amazing deep-sea **invertebrates**. Invertebrates are animals that do not have a backbone. Humans have a backbone. Worms do not. Worms are a type of invertebrate. Many of the strangest **marine** invertebrates live near **hydrothermal** vents. Life in this **habitat** leads to interesting **adaptations**.

Other worms in the sea

Giant tube worms are not the only worms in the deep sea. A Pompeii worm has a mostly gray body. It is covered with thin, red **gills**. The gills look a bit like a porcupine's quills. Pompeii worms are much smaller than giant tube worms. They are only about 10 centimeters (4 inches) long.

In two places at once

The worm's tail end sits in very hot water up to 80°C (176°F). This is the hottest water temperature animals can withstand. Only certain bacteria can live in hotter water. But the Pompeii worm's head rests in much cooler water. The Pompeii worm has **adapted** to life in two habitats at once!

This is a
Pompeii worm.

DEEP-SEA MUSSELS

Other interesting **invertebrates** make their home near **hydrothermal** vents. Like giant tube worms, some of these deep-sea dwellers have **bacteria** in their bodies. The bacteria take in vent gases such as hydrogen sulfide. They use chemicals (substances) in the gas to make **energy**. The deep-sea dwellers live off this energy.

Mussels are a type of **shellfish**. They have millions of **bacteria** inside their **gills**. The bacteria use energy from the vent gases and make food for the mussels. Mussels quickly move into new active vent sites. In fact, they are often the first creatures to show up there. They also can filter some food from the water. When the vent stops spewing gas, mussels can survive for a short time.

Some vent mussels grow as large as a person's hand.

Mussels cluster on rocks in the deep ocean.

Spider-mussel?

Mussels have a weird way of moving. They shoot out a strand, like a spider's web. The sticky strand latches onto a rock or other hard surface. Then the strand shortens and pulls the mussel along.

VENT CARNIVORES

Other animals living near **hydrothermal** vents get food in a different way. Some of these deep-sea creatures are **carnivores**. Carnivores are animals that eat other animals. Carnivores are also called **predators**. The animals they eat are called **prey**.

Crabs and shrimp are common vent predators. They feed on mussels that cluster near vents. Brachyuran crabs are round white crabs. They live near hydrothermal vents in the Pacific Ocean. They are fearsome predators, feeding on giant tube worms, mussels, shrimp, and even other crabs!

This round white crab feeds on vent mussels.

Scaleworms are covered with pink overlapping plates.

The scaleworm

Another common vent predator is the scaleworm. They do not look like any worms that live above ground! Scaleworms are flat and covered with overlapping pinkish-purple plates. The plates look a bit like pink potato chips. Scaleworms attach to black smokers, or underwater chimneys (see page 9). Scaleworms are also predators. They eat tiny **crustaceans** (shrimp-like animals) called copepods. When the vent stops working, carnivores like these cannot survive. They rely on other animals for food.

OTHER INTERESTING INVERTEBRATES

There are many amazing deep-sea **invertebrates**. Some live near vents, and others prowl the ocean floor.

Bloodybelly comb jelly

This strange creature looks a bit like a human heart. Bloodybellies range in color from purple to deep red, but all have a blood-red stomach. Scientists think the red color is an **adaptation**. Bloodybellies are predators. Some of the creatures they eat have **bioluminescence**. The striking red stomach hides the glow from these creatures. This keeps the bloodybelly from attracting predators itself.

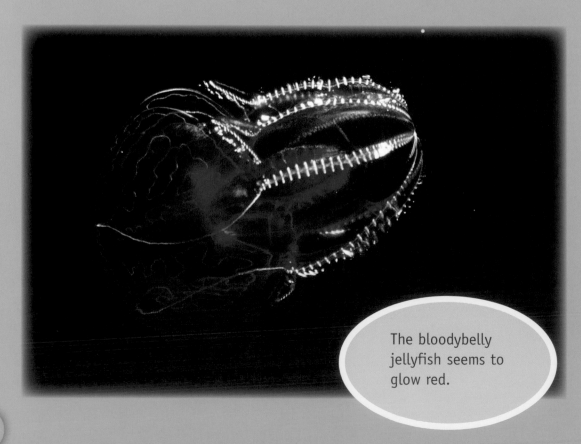

The bloodybelly jellyfish seems to glow red.

This glass sponge rests on the ocean floor.

Glass sponge

These strange animals look like white lace tubes. In fact, they are made of glass! The glass sponge forms thin layers of **silica**. Over time, the silica builds up into a complex structure.

Deep-sea squat lobster

This animal is not really a lobster at all. It is a type of crab. The squat lobster has very odd eating habits. It eats wood! Deep-sea squat lobsters munch on trees and other wood pieces that fall to the ocean floor. They even feast on shipwrecks!

EXPLORING THE DEEP SEA

Interesting **invertebrates** have **adapted** to life in the deep ocean. Humans have not. We cannot survive for long in the deep sea. The extreme cold and **pressure** are deadly to humans.

But there are many reasons to explore the deep sea. Scientists want to learn about the amazing animals that live there. But they cannot just swim down and look around. Even a wet suit and scuba gear are not enough. To explore the deep ocean, scientists need special vehicles and equipment.

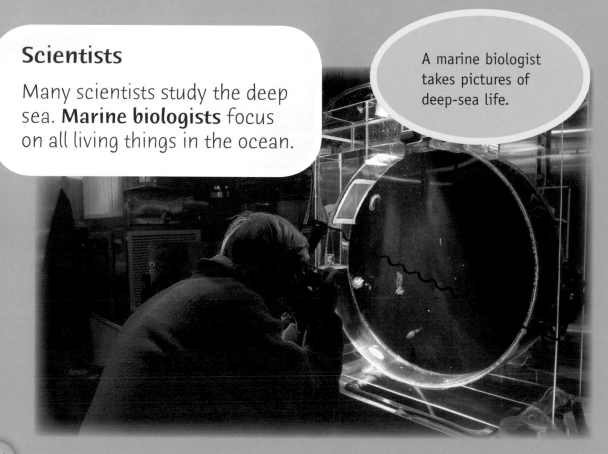

Scientists

Many scientists study the deep sea. **Marine biologists** focus on all living things in the ocean.

A marine biologist takes pictures of deep-sea life.

The bathysphere

One early deep-sea device was the bathysphere. It was a **sphere** made out of steel. Two people could fit inside. The steel held up to the intense water pressure. Inside was an oxygen tank so the people could breathe. In 1934 two scientists dove down to 923 meters (3,028 feet) below the surface. At the time, no one had been that far underwater.

This bathysphere (circa 1934) is being launched into the ocean.

MEET ALVIN

Today many cool tools help scientists explore the ocean floor. Deep-sea **submersibles** travel far underwater. They are like **submarines**, only smaller. Some submersibles stay attached to boats or submarines on the surface. Long hoses supply oxygen or power to the submersible. Others operate on their own. Scientists fit inside and control their movement.

A submersible named *Alvin* helped scientists explore **hydrothermal** vent systems. It made the first trip down to the vents in 1977. This submersible still makes more than 150 dives a year. It has been rebuilt many times. *Alvin* played a key role in the discovery of giant tube worms.

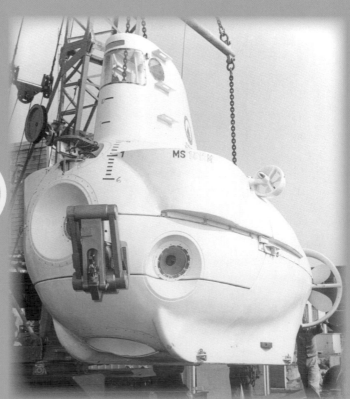

This is *Alvin*, the submersible.

Alvin has been rebuilt many times. It continues to help scientists explore the deep sea.

Sunken Sandwich

In 1968 scientists used steel cables to lower *Alvin* into the water. Suddenly the cables snapped. *Alvin* tumbled to the ocean floor. Luckily, the three crew members on board got out safely. But their lunch was trapped inside! Eleven months later, scientists brought *Alvin* back up to the surface. To their surprise, the bologna sandwiches had not spoiled! They were not exposed to sunlight or oxygen so far underwater.

SAVING THE DEEP SEA

The oceans are so large, it may seem like we do not need to worry about them. But we do.

Danger from people

The deep ocean is Earth's largest **habitat**. Today this unique habitat is at risk. **Pollution** threatens to change or harm the deep sea. (Pollution is harmful waste.) Human activity has led to **global warming**. Over time, the temperatures in the deep sea may change. This would upset the delicate balance of **hydrothermal** vent systems. Vent dwellers have **adapted** to the exact conditions there. If the conditions change, they may not survive.

The ocean is home to many amazing living things, such as these sea butterflies.

Pollution poses a major threat to the world's oceans.

More to explore

It is important to protect the deep ocean. There is still much to learn about it. We know little about many of the amazing animals that live there. Many deep-sea dwellers have not been discovered yet. Scientists know more about the surface of the moon than the deep sea!

GLOSSARY

adapt to change to fit an environment

adaptation feature developed over time that helps a living thing to survive in its environment

bacterium (pl. bacteria) living thing made up of a single cell

bioluminescence light given off by a living thing

carnivore animal that feeds only on other animals

chitin hard material found in the outer skeleton of invertebrates

crustacean living things with a hard exoskeleton, two pairs of antennae, and a pair of legs on each segment

energy power to move, change, or grow

gill organ that allows ocean dwellers to take in oxygen from the water

global warming changes in temperature that are taking place around the world

habitat place where a living thing lives. Living things adapt to their habitat.

hydrothermal having to do with hot water

invertebrate animal without a backbone

marine having to do with the ocean

marine biologist scientist who studies plants and animals in the ocean

pollution harmful waste

predator animal that eats other animals. Some deep-sea predators hunt for food along the ocean floor.

pressure force that pushes in all directions

prey animal that is eaten by other animals

shellfish sea dweller with a hard outer shell

spawning releasing eggs into the water to be fertilized

sperm male seed that fertilizes the egg

silica mineral used to make glass

sphere evenly round object like a ball

spring source of water that comes from the ground

submarine vehicle built to explore underwater

submersible small underwater craft

toxic poisonous

FIND OUT MORE

Books

Galko, Francine. *Classifying Invertebrates (Classifying Living Things)*. Heinemann Library: Chicago, 2009.

Lockyer, John. *Life in the Ocean Layers*. Huntington Beach, Calif.: Teacher Created Materials, 2008.

Weber, Valerie J. *Giant Tubeworms (Weird Wonders of the Deep)*. Milwaukee, Wis.: Gareth Stevens, 2005.

Websites

http://kids.nationalgeographic.com/kids/activities/new/ocean
Learn about the creatures that make their home in the ocean. You can also play games and do activities.

www2.scholastic.com/browse/article.jsp?id=3748096
Read about how scientists explore the deep ocean.

http://school.discoveryeducation.com/schooladventures/planetocean/tubeworm.html
This page gives information about the giant tube worm.

INDEX

DEC '77

3 0646 00296 1252

Riverhead Free Library
330 Court Street
Riverhead, New York 11901